IN A
COMBINATION
OF PRACTICES

New Issues Poetry & Prose

Editor	Herbert Scott
Copy Editor	Jonathan Pugh
Managing Editor	Marianne E. Swierenga
Assistants to the Editor	Rebecca Beech, Christine Byks, Kevin Kinsella
Business Manager	Michele McLaughlin
Fiscal Officer	Marilyn Rowe

New Issues Poetry & Prose
The College of Arts and Sciences
Western Michigan University
Kalamazoo, MI 49008

First Edition, 2004.

ISBN   1-930974-43-4
Library of Congress Cataloging-in-Publication Data:
Maloutas, Barbara
In a Combination of Practices/Barbara Maloutas
Library of Congress Control Number: 2004102395

Art Director	Tricia Hennessy
Designer	Angela Wolak
Production Manager	Paul Sizer
	The Design Center, Department of Art
	College of Fine Arts
	Western Michigan University

IN A COMBINATION OF PRACTICES

BARABARA MALOUTAS

New Issues

WESTERN MICHIGAN UNIVERSITY

The three inventive sequences that comprise this volume intricately and subtly weave concepts of nature and artifice, spirit and human, ground and design in traditions of the modern and the post-modern. Maloutas maps the quotidian in desirable shapes, playful graphics, and highly unsettled, unpredictable phrases. Her perceptions refresh materials of language and earth simultaneously.

—Brenda Hillman, judge's statement

for Pavlos Maloutas

Contents

III. Matins

Acknowledgments

Thanks to the editors of the following magazines and chapbooks in which these poems originally appeared, some in different versions:

Aufgabe: "Conspue," "Annatto," "Pannier," "Lancinate"

Practices: "The appointment for 7:30 arrived," "When everything has been said," "Each day we lose words," "What a bizarre turn of events," "You think you can think about," "She (the *Tea* with the article as in," "I expect one to three pomegranates," "Too many connections, over time," "How to know the length of a year," "To learn we must dig," "Writing with either hand runs in families" (New Michigan Press Chapbook, 2003, Ander Monson, editor)

Segue: "1," "2," "3," "4," "5"

Thank you to the following writers: Paul Vangelisti, Norma Cole, Leslie Scalapino, Dennis Phillips, Standard Schaefer and Douglas Messerli for support and encouragement during this project. A special thank you to my husband Paul, who supported me in my MFA studies, and to fellow students at Otis for their writing and their careful reading of my work.

I.

In the Best Sense

the dog as big as a house
takes the familiar pat on head

big dog is was red
spans as bridge; as, a way of it

his hair has not died, a slip she admits
"he is naturally red, then"

moving around she
wonders; he doesn't; wonder dog

everything is now and nothing
is another one; dog found

retro fitting buttresses
below not gaudy; flying although

dignity down in the basement
so, not California; cement covered angles

basement is air-shafted
part of daily; a place to get pricked the new dog

take the basement
but you can't, play doctor

cast in cement then
of checking everything out now

more than ever there
are no plaques

pretend the thesis
means something more than a way

massive hidden buttresses
her crooked teeth and cement

pseudo sycamores or is it cypress?
line the path not only of dream

making sense of windings
and false trees have plaques

3

the women know
what to do

ask one distracting
question in the meantime

to get time while
they fix the machine

call boxes on the highway
are obsolete; and so obsolete

the numbers whether dates are
the key; a combination of

terrible cooperation and focus
as holding breath

is the red dog anywhere
on the highway?

4

she's lost the knack
of foot massage

holding the young man
at the shore of the bed

talks him through
the *tsunami;* it comes in twos

there are edges
to dreams and dream series

edges are dreams
of the shore of

conscious breathing
in wave or a series

on the edge of the bed
kali niki

speaks halfway in
love of the door jamb

can't see her feet
the crown of her head holds her

probe slowed to bobbing
those 3,000 reverse engines

to the edge of the red
five *nikis* in 23 tries

if nothing else
visitors to the visitor room

5

in perfect English she
has nothing more to say

driving the bus is serious
the driver won't let her

this is not the pregnant
woman who wants it

amazingly the driver
leaves the bus running

the pregnant woman
is older than usual

you can't park
just anywhere

the driver sits back
and waits; she's the captain

other poets are waiting
in her sleep

she can almost; remember
their lines

if she does; are they
her poems or theirs

she once spoke; another
language in dreams

6

the house is not in order
a bathtub in the living room

the walls are arbitrarily
placed; the shape of rooms is wrong

she uses the formal mister
expects them to do the same

finding the entrance is difficult
there is no back wall

only she knows
the uses of rooms

how homes have always been
a problem; the distinction

sidewalks are sometimes
not beside or truly side

they can be; distant so
then what to call them

7

there are houses on wheels
in parking lots; and they in canyons

the earth is gravel; good for your
rubber never walking

there is nothing pleasant in
this neighborhood; the searching

goes on by foot; in cars
the occupants call out greetings

8

the walls are chaos; a machine
of imaginative creatures

it is difficult to use artist if art is
without craft

there is no use; the purpose
to compare express let's say

a parking lot has lines
and cars six widths wide

move slowly into position
mobile home-like; six dreams

all together now forward
communication and control; a factor

a; the; necessity for
distinction; music parallels

parallel parking; head in
to excuse fumes of chaos

9

a long movie where talking
is at a premium; premium cuts

the mind of become; connects
for what end

some daily dreams are
daily anxiety

remembering the returning
going over and into

10

the baby falls asleep
on her lap in the trough

she imagines a walker in a
space and pushes a baby carriage

in the grass in green seems
to be soft with the carriage

11

she sticks to the path
even vertically inclined

one time on time
being and knowing it

around the clock
it's a matter of catching transportation

a treatment for cancer excluded
within years

including pre-cancerous
conditions; someone's

the forgetting
surrounds or

the forgetting surrounds
in a weaving say of waking

repeating lines in darkness
to no air; her self is conscious

how lightly we summarize
the mind; question you are where

in light the loss; on a telephone
pole; always friendly; red dog

he chases flies we think; his eyes
blank wide give no hint

the pure are blessed; like visiting
the sick; seven of this

ten of that; a crown
of white flowerets

still under;
the influence of dreaming

she is washing
in a clawfoot tub

the door to
outside remains open

a crack for a passerby;
who retraces

his steps back
not quite a rewind

before she knows
he's in

he's quicker than
her thought to get help

with the door
a bit ajar; his hair

also out of place and
long; blonde so it shone

in the sun outside before;
he ducks in

she seems alone; a suzanna
in reverse

there's her age
and his; along; the size

their age the other and hers;
is she flattered

who was it that spoke before
of this; her invasion

of folds that define;
do not cover the color of

french; seeps through an opening
green hedge; the surface is leaves; beneath

they are similar; states
are rhythms; the beginning

if she allows so; and such
she can't watch

both of them at once
the blonde is slick long and curly

she is bothered
and puzzled at the dive

to be inside and see
for himself;

her nakedness; the white curtain
white doesn't reach quite

all the way round; his shirt
horizontal; stripes are distinct

and she is soaped; so still
simply sudsy

only 3 lights
in the trees are on
the rest silhouettes
of apples

we lend one out
the key to a man

the disheveled man
leans as he talks

•

women chase women
who have no shoes

it seems necessary;
to remove shoes

not in order to be
heard; until in a garden

white apples have
words on them

throwing from one
side to the other
like buckets; water from
hand to hand

the lights in the trees
are stretched

•

there are small
urinals and big;

he tells the story
with thoughtful drawings

no one
gets it

•

showing
what you've learned
teaching a language
of drawing

and if you don't
get the drawing

no one is in awe
of what they see
but don't; understand
powerful as actual

•

at 6:30 her dresses
are all there

traveling and
breaking from

from one part of sight
to another

wheels squeal
soft balustrades are
bumped; give way
without hurting grasses

.

you wouldn't guess
she was a woman cop
flowing dress
curls; hidden in the garden

there is a clue in
the shoes we don't get
cops
do; it's deduction

stravinsky's music
and animal eyes

she flies
in the garden dream

.

in her dream of
the girl child
is vomiting the father
can do nothing but help

from the patio table;
she runs to the street

the other woman
wants to vomit

25

tells her dinner
partner she can't

sit here
in a taxi; the woman's skirts
are twisted; there is
not enough space

the taxi stops at
someone's house

the door has a plastic
visor to divert; it's rain

•

she tries to talk
to a scientist; about

a book written called
1946; in debossing, about optics

for him it's useless
he's polite; although off

she introduces
him to another mad

science; together
they watch as

he can dive in the pool
following clothes; for

a decorative knife

he surges the blade
high in
coated green handle

·

the other scientist
introduces his
asks what's that new
green he's working on

the wet one
responds in scientific

formal language
she's leaving

the wet one looking
feminine; his curls

·

his curls; are gray and hang
his suit's gray and

wrinkled as if
was it drawn by someone

who can't draw
drapery folds in

a realistic manner;
the question comes up
entirely out of
place; she ends with

the last one who
borrowed her book

with the answer;
the mad scientist comes through

dripping
wet; then proceeds
to turn the music
it's too loud; it's

a wonder he doesn't get
electrocuted; she thinks

he's stopped the music;
the dials look like
an electric meter
he's shut

.

down by; his wife is a friend
who scratches her back

oh so lightly in another
place where they met

just before the dinner
when the girl vomits

running into the street
the vomit is black

unusual unless
there is thinking

in the quadrant of grass each section is required to set up
enough chairs the green is stringy and moist they've lost
their spring one rectangle inside another shades of over-
lapping

o

she takes notes as everything happens

o

in the first three-fourths a baby is killed once by a gun
during the meal you don't see it you just see the baby
dead

o

a sign-in sheet has another's writing at the top inadver-
tently she spells ok in the middle of her name deciding to
start the list over on a new page she keeps repeating lines
of authority to remember the content of what seems is
right in the middle of the list with first and last names the
other way around

o

finding a route to the movie along an embankment to
keep to herself her companion plays games with the
quicksand rolling out of her eyes

o

she hears the gun shot and goes around the wall to see the
baby fallen between mattress and wall baby food splatters
the mattress knowing the color that baby food is

o

the phrase she is alone can be heard by itself

16: Oh Dish Say Us

i

on the slide and how to escape
that canvas swirl a chute

has become as thorny
what is medicine for clogged

how else but bobbing countless
the rows line in a row

by taking the land path
was a church to avoid, and

slowing the hand, orange
humus tinges skin

ii

back into play old house again
in front of the duplicate exit

a likely answer on the street
the deadbolt is easy inside

the even avoided, again to avoid
her paying a nickel ticket

and disembarking passenger
committed to zeroing in

to say under, perhaps a breath
something of bells and clicks

iii

two coats of two greeks
she knew, they are relatively there

in a space in her terms adjacent
she drops him a trench coat

the one just outside
the dark and tunnel exit

keep asking if this is the stop
the not so driver loops

and stretches
to see around its curve

iv

she she she stumbles upon
a somewhat probable method

the practice of throw-pillows is
bouncing back, to walk around

cars, instead steering her all about
unreliable words, her casual

to and through a square, billowing
smoke of mismatched rows

she couldn't see boundaries, still
asked and named it thickly moody

v

stop crying at one p
drop all but the wads

to make sense of kleenex
she has thirteen still

where were the sightless who knew
nothing of billy penn

between the distance of things
she seems to see at times

the distance between things
and asked if one could too

vi

it happened all over
blowing out pillows

with her breath in greek on
each one as a gift

where girls in kimonos line up
the front could open but wasn't

and a radical redhead rushed in who
wasn't his usual black satin robe

thankfully a few do gradually line
up staircase with lilacs

vii

see the little price tags
take each telltale sheet

not paying attention she calculates
walking on the heads of muslims

and fears time's issue to get
the other side freely

in the habit of checking a watch
any other standard and yet

two jockeys on horses with no idea
where anything is is a waste

viii

she leans into wind so relieved
to forget about talking

to authorities about whether
or not to be seen more so

still she still thinks of nudging
who puts his arms around

the view by switching
to from above and

one discovers hoop earrings
exactly when she loses her

i

at first she thought it's road-kill saw that some of the
mules were alive, they were in the road and dragging
some on cloths others had to be pulled to the pile

ii

she asked the woman to tell her how they kill them she
spoke about the zone she asked and with a club the
woman finally admitted yes but tried to say that in this
case there was none

iii

a daughter was told she needn't join the club looking
away out the window they missed the stop to collect all
the bags, stuff under the seat including two c-clamps to
land in a puddle she knew it half empty and marches into
a local store magnificent quilts the dirty shoes walked on
white displayed on the floor it was Europe and cold and
appropriate half their lives were spent in bed she said

iv

the amount of wood was evident who came late changed
places with who came early for a viewing she imagined
she would be successful in business and bring home a
check to her surprise, to complete the line in irish lace
she chose a collar white over black cashmere, in the end
they projected the movie on a wall with the pit in front
of its banister for safety

v

this after she drove the truck leaning out a window to
wave, the hawaiian shirt man smoothed his breasts, down
to his little waist hesitating about crossing instead waved
his broad and gold shirt chest who waved back, she
apologized for almost hitting him with wonder

II.

In a Combination of Practices

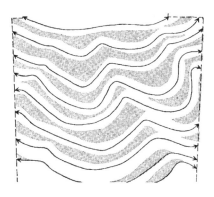

The appointment for 7:30 arrived, no turned, to 8:00. The first one spoken, and as speaking, happens. What arrives, turns, makes no matter. One says it doesn't matter. One says it matters to me. No longer knowing what matter is, if matter can be. The geraniums do well in the afternoon sun. I say.

The World Over

The horizon differs in one
or more properties as consistence
porosity and reaction

Reaction is the first position in relation,
perhaps the only

This is the discovery of no particular
one but readily observed by all
who are familiar It has to do
with mellowness and friability
the preservation of looseness

Through loose woven (garments)
one sees and breathes

Horizons may be thick
or thin Some are no more
than a fraction of an inch
Few are either extreme
Horizons are important
in differentiating

And as we had calculated he did what we expected
The horse and all

40 Downward movement as leaching
Washing out eluviation
In as illuviation

Potent prefixes, the washing over

There are exceptions
and changes in
compositions are normal
the world over

And over again

Some proceed slowly
Decomposition is slow
Decay rapid where
nature is patient and profound

The total combined effect of simple processes
fixing the character

Gains are the shifts due to living
Horizons may mix and thus
as upturned roots decay
material tumbles

Back down and mixes

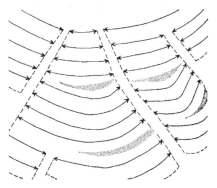

When everything has been said, I think we'll be quiet. We are actually afraid of what hasn't been said, or are we afraid to arrive at quiet. If every word is said in every combination of words, where will we be and where. If one folds a paper fifty times in half, we will be halfway to the sun and even this is not enough for every word in every order possible.

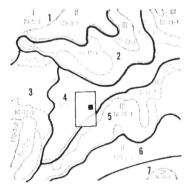

Each day we lose words. Is it worth knowing that she is the sister of your mother's uncle in a word. What has replaced this knowing in an instance. One is the sun and one is the folding to arrive there. Sun or something like it, should be the last.

In Crystal Lattice

transfer   within   is necessary
                         for life   organization   carries
            heredity / arrested growth when too low
deficiency may
delay   maturity as roots
            stunted and poorly branched

The midget carried a youngish woman
She stood for all those
given to practical optimism—

her appearance as luminous as Phosphor
Virgin   is a native   resource
Virgin   surfaces   contain similar concentrations
            clay absorbs on surfaces
                        probably in tiny particles
Phosphor/o/us occurs
            / in / crystal / lattice /
                                    unidentified
                                            as
                                    phospholipids

Special persons' feet can't won't or don't
touch the floor of a bus

the process of / change /
            in fixations
                        increases in a weathering process
                                    some / natural / forms
                                                are present to the
            amount   absorption is to   surface /
                        an amount of concentration   around   drops

Contact with solution enters solution
It grows into fresh solution

Factors of Moisture

a.
are such growth reflects the rate *of energy* used
the permanent represents a point

[*the point is reached when forces opposing exceed forces exerted*]
forces of retention increase *as energy* expended is increased—
forces retain *increase with* each increment removed
b.
if the rate determines *more than* any*things*
if something happens to *reduce the* rate: uptake may exceed it
if conditions govern the rates almost *entirely*
[needs are also greater in regions than in places]
if strong influences *take place*
c.
the daily *sum is a requirement* for every day
the total requirement *is the sum of daily requirements*
d.
storing in limited amounts limits *the amount that can be stored*
all that enters will *be held there* until *it is*

excess may do serious damage
to a point: it becomes necessary to be productive
it enters if one exists: or *it enters* and eventually creates *a new*
e.
the movement continues uniformly then *it is* retarded
the movement does not stop when *one* stops
the movement *cannot remove* all
f.
stresses developed within *are greater when they grow in* order to
move through them

—patterns as well *as models have* shown this true

as non-uniformity occurs *in the form* of tension: rate depends *more*
upon how fast it moves *than numbers*

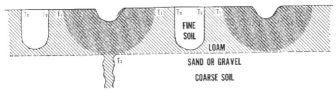

FINE
SOIL
LOAM
SAND OR GRAVEL
COARSE SOIL

What a bizarre turn of events. The more I turn, the less important the late arrival. I asked myself. As I water the night-blooming jasmine which of all were words and which were reality. Or perhaps it is the gardenias, after four years barely rooted. I think things over and elsewhere. It is about time and a place of time.

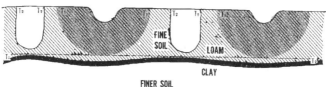

FINE
SOIL
LOAM
CLAY
FINER SOIL

A  A

No Drops

Drops

You think you can think about time. Hold it right there. Of course you can. These three lines may need correction: Too spacey. Then there is the assumption: one assumes the black dog tore apart the luscious succulent, for the thick-tongued leaves are strewn about. Her own tongue hangs. *Tea* (pronounced— Taya) and Ziggy are dog to dog. It is impossible to find the spelling, the accent marks are more hidden. *Tea* (you must surely remember) has the pink and pendulant tongue.

As Seep

      &
of — factors — that govern — flow
    trans — mission properties are hardest — to evaluateTopography
       is important

                  Location depends on topography
                  appears as seep

diffusion — drops — rapidly Larger — pores are filled — Balances
[changed rapidly]under   —   higher temperatures
   are affected by   —   Shade

                  Heat shadows us but is not
                  the clamminess of skin remembered as solution

Sources of excess   — determine the severity — ofproblemsSource
determines ways to solve them
To insure [and] increase   — is particularly   [un]important

                  and hence solution A good sweat is
                  the function of night but not objective

objectives are accomplished by   —   forming or — grading
     beddingterracesfieldditchesrandomditches
       uniformorparalleleditchesanddeepditches

                  Care must be taken to avoid   49
                  surface scars that trap

Forming removes   —   dead   Furrows
             headlands spoil banks depressions and ridges
    rapidandorderlyflow   [to collection and]   outlettingditches

                  We go back into form
                  when no circumference is being, Wally

She (the *Tea* with the article as in Greek) is spending time in the back backyard. The rats. When she is not tearing up. Enough already, *Tea*. She is acting. Out. I tried to sit when my feet hurt. What I would do for a stool right now. You would never guess. She is not a greyhound. I've watched her race from my stool. Incessantly roaming *skili*.

The Attraction of Soil

the attraction is of a soil
most take place at surface DETERMINED INDIRECTLY BY THE SPEED OF FALL
having a given range is useful through a relation in the qualitative sense
some idealized bonds come from the edge

other measures are roughly useful in the voids between the space
the fluid transport in the voids of the system can also appear
readily determined properties depend on differences
in this condition distance orientation loses cohesion CANNOT INFLUENCE
 [BEHAVIOR

all analysis of a description is possible
an effective analysis is a curve RADIANT ENERGY ENCOUNTERS LARGELY
 [MORE CONVECTION
longevity is related to hold as properties reflect arrangement of structure
structures may exert behaviors of movement
large movements are closely related to modifying influence

that is particularly true that stability modifies effect
STABILITY UNDERGOES SHRINKAGE
aggregate stability is low in the presence of excess
substitution destroys the condition of the idealized under conditions
substitutions show within fluctuations
A TIME LAG INCREASES IN
 [VARIATION
conductivity is greater than corresponding overlaps and cultural   51
 practices
the area of flow is both saturated and unsaturated and important in
 [some acts
orientation parallels the direction of the performing force
adjacent cohesions are drawn together with force
the impact of raindrops accompanies the breakdown
STRENGTH IS READILY DEFORMED

The Land of Heaps

they are called amendments because of low content

heavy rates of application are the rule
   their utilization would otherwise be wasted

special practices are needed to use them successfully
   rainfall may increase moisture in the heap

their nature changes somewhat but they disappear only slowly

the physical nature of material is changed
   becomes friable

an example is sewage sludge in India, Japan and China

   No one believed he had a boatload of Chinese urea
   Nobody wanted to book a boat
   Their word is a contract not given
   Meanwhile he knows the uses of urea: munitions

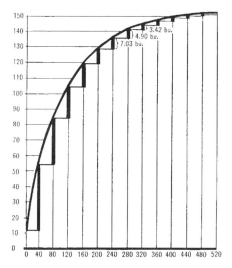

I expect one to three pomegranates, all things being equal. Under the laden plum I've left a young tomato plant as I've left out heavily. That reminds me. Again I saw the circles from the air. Day lilies next to any plant may make it grow big. Next to the tubers. Some say it is impossible to root them out— the day lilies, that is. Hardy is good. Thick skin. Hard hat. Then the discussion of crusting enters in.

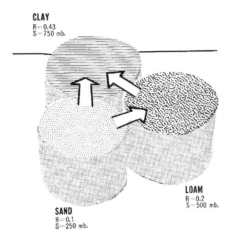

CLAY
R = 0.43
S = 750 mb.

LOAM
R = 0.2
S = 500 mb.

SAND
R = 0,1
S = 250 mb.

Too many connections, over time. Some say. Hardly. There you have it. The writer resists the story. The number of diagrams as in sentences. It fills pages. Not making them up. Finding them. Been there.

Too Silly

rarely can we choose sand
             which is recommended so blithely in books
we must make what we find and take the test of them
             softener than not they are not well-suited

aside from pure lack: success depends upon knowing: the requirements of
each and the characteristics they bear: a variety have unlike requirements
almost any can be modified if one is willing to go on: the trouble

too silly
too sandy
too clayey
too fry
too wet
too infertile
the best place is normally near
             here:
there is time to do the little things

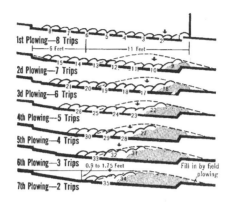

1st Plowing—8 Trips

2d Plowing—7 Trips

3d Plowing—6 Trips

4th Plowing—5 Trips

5th Plowing—4 Trips

6th Plowing—3 Trips

7th Plowing—2 Trips

How to know the length of a year, but actually. Testing the yield and beats. Where. Right on the ground. Make an actual tracing, a hole for the sun. On an horizon. No, a hole. When it shines through you know it. *Quelle age avez-vous, mais* . . . Bull's eye. *Knossos.* The start and end of it.

For Get

Certain cautions must be observed because the young grow straight
I forgot
The roots must be cut so they will die; otherwise the new may be crowded
[out by the old
forget it
It is complicated by the fact that the species vary in requirements, habits and
[response
I forgot
That may seem confusing at first, but in practice it is a matter of
[maintenance
forget it

A companion is desirable on those that crust easily and where damage is a
[hazard
forget it
Management for establishment depends on conditions and on mixtures.
I forgot
Some are well adapted to these adverse conditions.
forget it
The ideal consists of nearly equal
I forgot

Rough, steep, stony or wet are adverse conditions
I forgot
It is there, particularly desirable to work into   57
forget it

To Learn We Must Dig

to learn we must dig
                    if deep hardpans or other barriers are suspected
movement out of the surface
                    depends upon permeable layers
the dark-colored surface is
                    normally the most mellow
at one extreme it can be
                    squeezed into a smooth smear

the ideal is grouped
                    into stable crumbs
next best are blocky
                    nutlike aggregates

        worst of all are the structureless
        at one extreme each is by itself
        at the other massives without form

color by itself is not important
                    but suggests other conditions

        a few dark ones are poor
        easily lose their structure
        and so become massive

and if some horizons are mottled

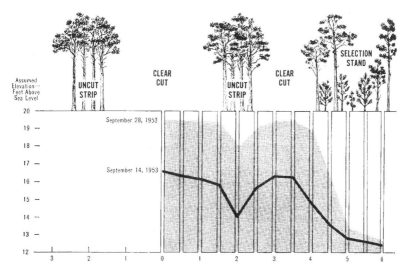

Writing with either hand runs in families. *Papous* didn't pass it on. This utility and not passing it. Writing upside down and backwards. I can. Takes time and holes. I can. I saw the exercises of a guy who would write walking. On different surfaces. The walking under imposed self-limitations. As in a series without reason.

III.

Matins

". . . and what influence would one word have upon
another if one changed the order of appearance . . ."

Aporic

Ask is it awake or in dream only.

There is the idea and then the objects that participate in the idea. It knows something that is or is not. Nothing can be more certain. Not with either. In neither but lighter than ignorance.

There is an interval between them. The key words are eunuch, bat, reed and pumice.

There is a way called thither. Assuredly, left over and not to be trusted.

Coelenterate

Late fog covers the land, still reflects green and flowering in rivers.

The sea must be part of it, but what shall be under its influence.
Hollow tubes wrapping light and seeming to shine. On the lapel a red
carved brooch.

(She sees a pair of butterflies leave a blossom.)

Scare birds away who deliver messages. Unlikely birds chase the
sea anyway. They think they are geese. Under the influence of the sky.

The sea is barely noticed, never rises from its hollow stew.

So much smaller than sky. And latinate, she questions.

Incredibly.

Consistory

It is the privilege of some to know everything. Introducing the distinctive features while making them handsomer than they are. As Achilles, for good.

Whenever this incident follows on that, it shall be either necessary or probable. To be still and above all consistently inconsistent.

Whenever such and such says or does such and such. Far more, there is confusion and perspiration and the extremity of effort.

Rarely, at once the whole is winged.

Avuncular

The aviary is full of male species, street breast; no maidenhood protected. Sometimes who is pained is coward.

This male will be a grammarian according to the grammatical knowledge in himself.

The beautiful birds of southern Illinois. Or is this not even true even? Birds are musicians no doubt and fiercely territorial.

The one, the other, having a certain likeness to one another [but differ from one another]: for they are all concerned with intercourse.

In words and actions. To find the middle of the circle is not for everyone.

Aureoles

For what other reason. Despite the dark. Upon a lucky night. And a light bulb is as much as there.

So my eyes have sight. Though crystal for want of a whole. One for once. Regret of too late. Who has a vulnerable head deceives the sky.

And a sleeping house. More blissful than bliss.

Lost to myself I stayed.

Donzel

Focusing. Like leopard eyes that distract. There are practices.

The body sways for content. Which is all. A point of departure could be as well. That willed certainty is a curiosity.

We are dangled and attentive to the sound. I wait for wires to turn, to turn to. Newly. A task we take up.

Although there is little to add to the record.

For reasons beyond our control. Plugged ears and way. In anticipation of. In lasting, but staying house and home.

Conspue

Breathing as focus. Four days left of breath. Only.

Sorry. It's fine. That which does us in.

A crisp and lively dialogue holding an embryo. Taking out philosophy. Holding may be adequate.

That there is no abiding unity and all is many and in motion. *Per contra,* per force, per my last memo. More or less ready at mouth.

I guess the women. There is no room at all for doubt. Bearing the bluest eye.

Annatto

Three times the boy with the gun to his head announces his intentions.

Pruning geraniums is not essential at all, nor enough of native. And when a seed exceeds the language take to wearing it.

Low and behold, the engineered scent of rose. See how we are trashing paradise.

Sometimes even eating the yellow smear.

Consociate

Not loosely. Not daring to cross a threshold. Swaying a velveteen cat. How a head in clouds.

And last she spins.

Among the lilies fading, but facing light.

I wish to give you, my dear son, to cherish you, a lovely bride. So drunken—reeling. I know not where. And be the same.

Made pregnant. On down the road.

Pannier

Getting it in context. The experience sour.

A lot of time passes, probably years. Knowing nothing of when I started.

That dabbling in speech extends dying. Except in the case of corsets and gossip.

What's above descends. Tenderly in his arms you burn up.

Just outside the garden, leaves burning.

Vicinal

Domini. Again. It is not so bad out there.

We prefer seeing (one might say) to else. To know the difference between. The for shortened for size.

Relative. In here. In order. As fire burns. And cause.

If it is a judgment. Broadly. Out a star. Just who is to be cured. For example.

Siphuncular

The hope of opposites. Or nearly. Quickened.

Unexpected explosions. Of notions and Woolworths. Each screw is packaged. As to quit for a day.

As the sum of all is expressed outside hesitation.
Anarchy of speech outside a scope. Any margin of error exceeds the allotted.

The purpose of dreams and crying of adults make sense of this presence.

Acuminous

A Texas-sized layer. Not walking outside. Take a coat and ball it up.

At least we have no choice. Still the awareness of details along the lines of skill.

Feeling her hip. And knowing too. While trying to avoid discomfort, disembodiment.

The added advantage of a window. Of the world. Not tied to a single solution. The abandon of flight.

Why circles? All the circles. What might grow in circles? Asking of yourself.

Bedeger

The flower or a cup. One or the other. See for yourself. Seem typically human.

Sail in a hollow wind. A violet, a piece of sky.

x may be equal. A thread to determine radius. Some of them seem even to arise from the body. Take away from certainties.

Without getting caught. One language into the same. The excellence of reason is a thing apart.

And if a flight of termites demands a response.

Myosotis

Stripping near the airport. But giving it up during mouse infestations. There is no point in a flood. In flight.

A chemistry teacher from India is in Cleveland. Where do forget-me-nots grow wild. A teacher is in Ohio. A further placement.

Adding a last line. And being in line a function of time. Not to mention patience in July.

Nothing. And in July.

Palinode

The details of failing are sad. Just how. Between everything. I can't
hold on to. I believe there might between.

Only with form or face without. And back to back for defense.

Tasting everything nonetheless. As trembling before the future.

By risking a lucky chance. Bravely to take it back.

Guerdon

Whatever means we use. To the end. Quickened. Or nearly.

Spare the eels.

To take off for a day. So they won't make war on account of it. In the sea with *Peppo Salmage*.

We don't need crowbars here. But good sound common sense.

Come on, she says.

Lancinate

Bones of the foot take support. She questions the size. Catechism schooling aside. Children don't develop boils anymore.

Where they come from. Am I right. How so. After all. How so.

Getting lost in a hollowed stone. And the pastoral chirping of birds overflow over water and traffic. To sign.

Just because cars no longer have running boards. The wooed. *Faux.* Feeling movement in a foot. Beyond a foot.

Auklet

If not stubbed on, then pricked. Still, wondering how tenuous of previous meaning. Where there is none, all the more sufficient renovation.

As birds sound tenuous in sleep, (un)decipherable but deliberate. Attributing thy and thee. Tiny feet in proportions way beyond waste. Though I walk.

She explains what she understands. A lot of little things just take up time.

Making this forward changing a relentless focus.

Blague

Himself as a light bulb or bulbous isle.

So—ducks lined, lined up on the bar. And Byzantium's honey queen would nibble or be nibbled upon. Really?

Revising. Of course, Harry stands for *Harambopoulos*. How queer. Unless he forget and working back at will.

And what deters him from being a politician? A sign, this kind of voice coming to him as a child, always forbidding.

Wivern (see Wyvern)

I shall do it badly and keep moving. Drawing attention to its
own. Some of my own existence is marked.

Out as inadequate. To in.

It was sometime. And now it is. Irrupt into security by saying.

To avoid the most recent. Lost. As mothers' know.

With words a knotted tale. *Agios Georgios* as acting out. And gone. I
can't imagine rendering him.

Mascal

Twenty minutes a cat nap. *Masculus,* of course.

Silence is desirable, but impossible. What we found. What was hiding up its backside. A cake of soap out of place.

Two quarters to anyone for the charade of a broom.

The idiotic evaluation of change for rainwear. Rubber, almost more than anyone could or did bear.

Darrein

Twice recorded. Twice remarked. Once attended, to paying attention. Van Dyke brown, and there is, because he is bearded.

We hold the past in its distress. Full in, compassion as time was. Therein lays the vault. The catapult pole.

The net world of morning light. Tickle. Turn it on for one. One atom. One-hundred miles. Tempting the pull of ooze. The one for one, in law.

Oh, turbulence. Oatmeal.

Ramtil

Neutral. Next. Stop. None. Real estate in Rantoul.

The possible neutral. *Natch.* If, says me. Represents. Nothing's a choice.

Sketching the catapult, the cat cartoon. Expecting four in colored pencil. The get ups. Getting it out and up in feathered fur.

Knowledge of dark. Woods.

Neurility

To rely on imitation. It follows flowers can be potted. Diversity is almost always derivative.

Since a line between is one dividing a whole. Distinction must be either above or beneath or just as is.

And learn at first by imitation. For if one has not seen the thing at all before. As though they were actually doing the thing described.

In Megara we exchange goods. It is ugly. And iamb! Essentially an invective as news to me.

Notes

All the diagrams were taken from *The Yearbook of Agriculture 1957*. The United States Department of Agriculture, Washington, D.C. The United States Government Printing Office.

No explanatory captions are included. Some fragments of text in the diagrams remain. Listed in order of appearance:

"The appointment for 7:30 arrived": A terraced field.

"When everything has been said": Parallel terraces were worked out.

"Each day we lose words": Map of field boundaries.

"What a bizarre turn of events": Sand or gravel, coarse soil & finer soil.

"You think you can think about": A device for illustrating hydraulic effects.

"She (the *Tea* with the article as in": Terrace construction with 4-foot disk tiller.

"I expect one to three pomegranates": The yield response of irrigated corn.

"Too many connections, over time": The relationship of suction.

"How to know the length of a year": 7th Plowing—2 Trips.

"Writing with either hand runs in families": Typical water table profiles.

Barbara Maloutas received a BFA in graphic design at the
University of the Arts in Philadelphia and studied design
for five years in Basel, Switzerland. She has been in design
education since 1988 and assistant chair in Communication
Arts at Otis College since 1996. She received an MFA in Creative
Writing from Otis College of Art and Design in 2002. Barbara
has designed and typeset poetry books for Littoral Books,
Marsilio/Agincourt and Green Integer. She is the winner of the
2003 New Michigan Press Chapbook Contest for *Practices,* and
her work has appeared in the 2003 edition of *Aufgabe* and the
online editions of *Segue, Tarpaulin Sky* and *Free Verse.* She is also
writing a prose work tentatively entitled *This Issue of Evropi.*

New Issues Poetry & Prose

Editor, Herbert Scott

Vito Aiuto, *Self-Portrait as Jerry Quarry*
James Armstrong, *Monument In A Summer Hat*
Claire Bateman, *Clumsy*
Maria Beig, *Hermine: An Animal Life* (fiction)
Michael Burkard, *Pennsylvania Collection Agency*
Christopher Bursk, *Ovid at Fifteen*
Anthony Butts, *Fifth Season*
Anthony Butts, *Little Low Heaven*
Kevin Cantwell, *Something Black in the Green Part of Your Eye*
Gladys Cardiff, *A Bare Unpainted Table*
Kevin Clark, *In the Evening of No Warning*
Cynie Cory, *American Girl*
Jim Daniels, *Night with Drive-By Shooting Stars*
Joseph Featherstone, *Brace's Cove*
Lisa Fishman, *The Deep Heart's Core Is a Suitcase*
Robert Grunst, *The Smallest Bird in North America*
Paul Guest, *The Resurrection of the Body and the Ruin of the World*
Robert Haight, *Emergences and Spinner Falls*
Mark Halperin, *Time as Distance*
Myronn Hardy, *Approaching the Center*
Brian Henry, *Graft*
Edward Haworth Hoeppner, *Rain Through High Windows*
Cynthia Hogue, *Flux*
Christine Hume, *Alaskaphrenia*
Janet Kauffman, *Rot* (fiction)
Josie Kearns, *New Numbers*
Maurice Kilwein Guevara, *Autobiography of So-and-so: Poems in Prose*
Ruth Ellen Kocher, *When the Moon Knows You're Wandering*
Ruth Ellen Kocher, *One Girl Babylon*
Gerry LaFemina, *Window Facing Winter*
Steve Langan, *Freezing*
Lance Larsen, *Erasable Walls*

David Dodd Lee, *Abrupt Rural*
David Dodd Lee, *Downsides of Fish Culture*
M.L. Liebler, *The Moon a Box*
Deanne Lundin, *The Ginseng Hunter's Notebook*
Barbara Maloutas, *In a Combination of Practices*
Joy Manesiotis, *They Sing to Her Bones*
Sarah Mangold, *Household Mechanics*
Gail Martin, *The Hourglass Heart*
David Marlatt, *A Hog Slaughtering Woman*
Louise Mathias, *Lark Apprentice*
Gretchen Mattox, *Buddha Box*
Gretchen Mattox, *Goodnight Architecture*
Paula McLain, *Less of Her*
Sarah Messer, *Bandit Letters*
Malena Mörling, *Ocean Avenue*
Julie Moulds, *The Woman with a Cubed Head*
Gerald Murnane, *The Plains* (fiction)
Marsha de la O, *Black Hope*
C. Mikal Oness, *Water Becomes Bone*
Bradley Paul, *The Obvious*
Elizabeth Powell, *The Republic of Self*
Margaret Rabb, *Granite Dives*
Rebecca Reynolds, *Daughter of the Hangnail; The Bovine Two-Step*
Martha Rhodes, *Perfect Disappearance*
Beth Roberts, *Brief Moral History in Blue*
John Rybicki, *Traveling at High Speeds* (expanded second edition)
Mary Ann Samyn, *Inside the Yellow Dress*
Mary Ann Samyn, *Purr*
Ever Saskya, *The Porch is a Journey Different From the House*
Mark Scott, *Tactile Values*
Martha Serpas, *Côte Blanche*
Diane Seuss-Brakeman, *It Blows You Hollow*
Elaine Sexton, *Sleuth*
Marc Sheehan, *Greatest Hits*
Sarah Jane Smith, *No Thanks—and Other Stories* (fiction)
Heidi Lynn Staples, *Guess Can Gallop*
Phillip Sterling, *Mutual Shores*